Mindful Wealth

Mindful Wealth

Matthew Petchinsky

Mindful Wealth: The New Blueprint for Financial Freedom
By: Matthew Petchinsky

Introduction

The Gateway to Wealth: Why Mindset and Mindfulness Are Your Greatest Assets

When people think about wealth, their minds often race to visions of opulent lifestyles, overflowing bank accounts, and the freedom to indulge in every desire. But what if I told you that the true foundation of wealth isn't built on external assets but rather on something far more personal and transformative: your mindset? In fact, the journey to financial success starts not with money in your pocket, but with clarity and purpose in your mind. This introduction will explore how cultivating the right mindset and embracing mindfulness can radically alter your relationship with money and set you on a sustainable path toward prosperity.

Why Wealth Starts with the Right Mindset

Wealth is often misunderstood as a destination—a finish line to cross when you've accumulated enough material possessions. In reality, wealth is a state of being, a reflection of how you think, feel, and act in alignment with your goals and values. The truth is, your mindset determines the extent of your financial success because it governs how you approach opportunities, handle challenges, and interact with the world around you.

A wealth-oriented mindset requires shifting away from limiting beliefs such as "Money is the root of all evil" or "I'll never be good with finances." These deeply ingrained ideas can act as invisible barriers, keeping you stuck in cycles of scarcity. Instead, adopting a growth mindset—a belief that you can learn, adapt, and grow—creates space for innovation, resilience, and optimism in your financial journey.

Think about it: How often do you find yourself saying, "I can't afford this," instead of asking, "How can I afford this?" This subtle shift in language reflects a fundamental difference in mindset. A scarcity mindset sees limitations, while an abundance mindset seeks possibilities.

By learning to recognize and reframe your internal narratives, you begin to open doors to opportunities you may have previously overlooked.

How Mindfulness Transforms Your Relationship with Money

Mindfulness—the practice of being fully present in the moment—has long been heralded as a tool for reducing stress and increasing mental clarity. But its applications extend far beyond meditation cushions and yoga mats. When applied to your financial life, mindfulness becomes a powerful lens through which you can examine your habits, decisions, and emotional triggers around money.

For many, money is fraught with anxiety. Whether it's worrying about bills, feeling guilty for spending, or experiencing shame over past financial mistakes, these emotions can cloud judgment and lead to reactive decisions. Mindfulness, however, teaches you to pause, observe, and respond with intention rather than impulse.

Imagine the simple act of making a purchase. Instead of swiping your card on autopilot, mindfulness encourages you to ask:

- Do I really need this?
- How does this purchase align with my long-term goals?
- Am I spending out of joy, or am I trying to fill an emotional void?

This practice of intentional reflection helps you break free from the cycle of mindless spending and cultivates a deeper awareness of the value of your money. Over time, mindfulness allows you to foster a healthier relationship with your finances—one built on respect, purpose, and control.

The Intersection of Mindset and Mindfulness

While mindset provides the framework for how you view wealth, mindfulness equips you with the tools to make conscious choices in alignment with that vision. Together, they form the foundation for true financial freedom. A wealth-oriented mindset might inspire you to pursue new income streams or investments, while mindfulness ensures you remain grounded, deliberate, and focused on what truly matters.

Consider the countless stories of lottery winners or sudden inheritors of wealth who quickly lose their fortunes. Their downfall isn't a lack of resources; it's the absence of the mindset and mindfulness needed to manage their money wisely. On the other hand, there are countless examples of individuals who started with very little yet built substantial wealth through persistence, self-awareness, and disciplined decision-making.

A New Way Forward

This book isn't just about numbers, budgets, or financial strategies—although those are important and will be covered. It's about equipping you with the mental and emotional tools necessary to thrive in the financial world. By the end of this journey, you'll understand that wealth is not an external treasure to be pursued but an internal state to be cultivated.

Whether you're starting from scratch, trying to break free from debt, or aiming to amplify your existing wealth, this book will guide you toward a new way of thinking about money. Together, we'll unlock the secrets of combining a wealth-oriented mindset with mindful practices, empowering you to achieve not just financial success, but a life of purpose, balance, and abundance.

So, let's begin this transformative journey. The wealth you seek is already within you—waiting to be unleashed.

Chapter 1: The Money Mindset Shift

Breaking Free from Limiting Beliefs About Money and Creating a Positive Financial Outlook

The journey to financial success begins with a single, often-overlooked step: the decision to transform how you think about money. Before you can build wealth, you must first identify and break free from the mental blocks and limiting beliefs that have held you back. This chapter will guide you through the process of shedding negative money mindsets and creating a positive, empowering financial outlook that sets the foundation for sustainable prosperity.

Breaking Free from Limiting Beliefs About Money

Limiting beliefs about money are deeply ingrained thoughts or assumptions that restrict your ability to achieve financial success. These beliefs often originate from childhood, shaped by cultural narratives, family dynamics, or past experiences. While they may seem harmless or even rational, they can act as invisible chains, keeping you trapped in cycles of financial struggle.

Common Limiting Beliefs About Money

1. **"Money is the root of all evil."**
   This belief instills the idea that wealth is inherently immoral or corrupting. People who hold this mindset may unconsciously sabotage their financial growth to avoid guilt or judgment.

2. **"I'll never be wealthy."**
   This belief fosters a sense of resignation and helplessness. It convinces you that financial success is unattainable, regardless of effort or strategy.

3. **"I'm bad with money."**
   Often rooted in past mistakes, this belief reinforces self-doubt and discourages you from learning or improving your financial skills.

4. **"Rich people are greedy or selfish."**
   This belief creates an internal conflict where you associate wealth with undesirable traits, making it harder to pursue financial success without guilt.

5. **"I have to work extremely hard to make money."**
   While effort is important, this belief often equates wealth with burnout and ignores the role of smart planning, creativity, and leverage.

Identifying Your Limiting Beliefs

The first step in overcoming limiting beliefs is recognizing them. Take a moment to reflect on the following questions:

- What were you taught about money growing up?
- How do you feel when you think about wealthy people?
- Do you believe financial success is possible for you? Why or why not?
- What patterns do you notice in your financial decisions?

Once you've identified these beliefs, write them down. Seeing them on paper can help you confront their irrationality and begin the process of replacing them with empowering alternatives.

Reframing Limiting Beliefs

Reframing is the practice of replacing negative beliefs with positive, constructive ones. For each limiting belief you've identified, challenge its validity and rewrite it as a statement of possibility:

- **Old belief:** "Money is the root of all evil."
- **New belief:** "Money is a tool that can amplify good or bad, depending on how it's used."
- **Old belief:** "I'm bad with money."
- **New belief:** "I'm learning to manage money wisely and improve my financial skills every day."

By consistently repeating and acting on these reframed beliefs, you can gradually rewire your mindset for financial success.

Creating a Positive Financial Outlook

Once you've addressed the mental blocks, the next step is to cultivate a mindset of optimism and abundance. A positive financial outlook isn't about ignoring challenges or pretending everything is perfect; it's about approaching your financial life with hope, resilience, and a proactive attitude.

The Power of Gratitude

Gratitude is one of the simplest yet most effective ways to shift your financial mindset. When you focus on what you already have, rather than what you lack, you train your brain to recognize opportunities and appreciate progress.

Action Step: Start a financial gratitude journal. Each day, write down three things you're grateful for related to your financial life, such as:

- The ability to pay your bills.
- A new opportunity to earn money.
- A lesson learned from a financial mistake.

Over time, this practice can help you build a healthier relationship with money.

Visualizing Financial Success

Visualization is a powerful tool for creating a positive financial outlook. By imagining your financial goals as already achieved, you program your mind to seek the actions and opportunities needed to make them a reality.

Action Step: Spend five minutes each morning visualizing your ideal financial life. Picture yourself living in financial freedom—what does it look like? How does it feel? Who are you helping or inspiring with your wealth?

This daily practice reinforces your commitment to your goals and keeps you motivated.

Setting Empowering Goals

A positive financial outlook thrives on clear, actionable goals. Rather than vague aspirations like "I want to be rich," focus on specific, measurable objectives:

- Pay off $5,000 in debt within six months.
- Save $10,000 for an emergency fund in one year.
- Earn an additional $1,000 per month through a side hustle.

When setting these goals, break them into smaller milestones and celebrate each victory along the way. This approach builds momentum and reinforces a sense of accomplishment.

The Ripple Effect of a Positive Money Mindset

Transforming your money mindset doesn't just impact your financial life—it ripples into every aspect of your existence. A confident, optimistic approach to money can lead to:

- Better decision-making under pressure.
- Improved relationships, as financial stress decreases.
- Greater willingness to take calculated risks and pursue opportunities.

As you cultivate this mindset, you'll notice that your relationship with money becomes less about fear or scarcity and more about empowerment and growth. You'll begin to see money as a tool, not a barrier—something to be managed and multiplied, not feared or hoarded.

Actionable Steps to Begin Your Money Mindset Shift Today

1. **List Your Limiting Beliefs:** Write down every negative thought you have about money.
2. **Reframe Each Belief:** Replace it with a positive, empowering statement.
3. **Start a Gratitude Journal:** Focus on what's working well in your financial life.
4. **Visualize Daily:** Spend a few minutes imagining your financial goals as already achieved.
5. **Set and Track Goals:** Create specific, realistic financial objectives and measure your progress.

In conclusion, shifting your money mindset is the first and most crucial step on the path to wealth. By breaking free from limiting beliefs and embracing a positive financial outlook, you lay the groundwork for a prosperous and fulfilling life. This transformation isn't just about accumulating wealth—it's about becoming the person who can manage, grow, and enjoy it with confidence and purpose.

Chapter 2: Mindful Money Habits
Small Daily Practices to Manage Wealth and How to Track Spending Without Stress

Building wealth isn't just about big financial decisions; it's about the consistent, mindful habits you cultivate every day. These small, intentional actions serve as the building blocks for long-term financial stability and growth. In this chapter, we will explore practical and stress-free ways to integrate mindful money habits into your daily routine, with a special focus on tracking spending and managing wealth without feeling overwhelmed.

Small Daily Practices to Manage Wealth

Developing wealth-building habits is like planting seeds; with regular attention and care, they grow into a thriving financial garden. Here are some small but powerful daily practices to help you manage your wealth effectively:

1. Begin with a Daily Money Check-In

Set aside five to ten minutes each day to review your finances. This simple practice helps you stay aware of your spending, saving, and financial goals without letting things pile up.

Action Step:

- Check your bank account balance and recent transactions.
- Review any pending bills or upcoming expenses.
- Reflect on how your spending aligns with your goals for the day.

2. Set a Daily Spending Intention

Before you start your day, decide how much you intend to spend and what you'll spend it on. By setting a clear intention, you avoid impulsive purchases and maintain focus on your financial priorities.

Action Step:

Write down your spending intention in a notebook or your phone. For example:

- "Today, I will spend $15 on groceries and nothing else."
- "I'll only use cash for today's transactions."

3. Practice Conscious Spending

Mindful spending is about pausing before every purchase to ensure it aligns with your values and goals. This habit helps you differentiate between needs, wants, and emotional impulses.

Action Step:

Ask yourself these questions before making a purchase:

- Is this something I truly need or want?
- Does it align with my financial goals?
- How will I feel about this purchase tomorrow or next week?

4. Automate Your Savings

Automation is a powerful tool for building wealth effortlessly. By setting up automatic transfers to your savings or investment accounts, you ensure consistent progress toward your financial goals.

Action Step:

- Choose a percentage of your income (e.g., 10%) to transfer automatically to savings.
- Use apps or bank features to set up recurring transfers.

5. Celebrate Small Wins

Acknowledging your financial progress, no matter how small, reinforces positive habits and keeps you motivated.

Action Step:

At the end of each week, reflect on your financial achievements, such as sticking to your budget or saving an extra $20. Treat yourself to a non-monetary reward, like a relaxing evening or a favorite activity.

How to Track Spending Without Stress

For many people, tracking expenses feels like a chore. The good news is that it doesn't have to be stressful or time-consuming. By adopting simple, mindful methods, you can gain clarity over your finances while keeping the process manageable and even enjoyable.

1. Keep It Simple

The key to effective tracking is to avoid overcomplication. Choose a method that fits your lifestyle and stick with it. Whether it's a notebook, an app, or a spreadsheet, simplicity is your ally.

Action Step:

Start by categorizing your expenses into broad groups like:

- Essentials (e.g., rent, utilities, groceries)
- Non-Essentials (e.g., dining out, entertainment)
- Savings and Investments

Track only the categories that matter most to you, rather than every single transaction.

2. Use Technology to Your Advantage

Apps and online tools can automate much of the tracking process, saving you time and effort. Many apps connect to your bank accounts and categorize transactions automatically.

Popular Apps to Consider:

- Mint: Tracks spending, budgets, and goals.
- YNAB (You Need A Budget): Helps you allocate every dollar to a specific purpose.
- PocketGuard: Shows how much you can safely spend after accounting for bills and savings.

Action Step:

Choose one app that suits your needs and spend 10 minutes setting it up. Let the app handle the tracking while you focus on mindful decision-making.

3. Schedule Weekly Reviews

Rather than checking every transaction obsessively, schedule a dedicated time once a week to review your spending. This approach reduces stress and allows you to catch any discrepancies or overspending.

Action Step:

- Choose a specific day and time for your review (e.g., Sunday evening).
- During the review, compare your actual spending to your budget and adjust as needed.

4. Embrace the Power of Cash

Using cash for discretionary spending can be an effective way to limit expenses without needing constant tracking. When you physically hand over cash, you're more aware of how much you're spending compared to swiping a card.

Action Step:

- Withdraw a set amount of cash at the beginning of the week.
- Use only this cash for non-essential purchases.

5. Reflect on Emotional Triggers

Mindless spending often stems from emotional triggers like stress, boredom, or social pressure. By identifying these triggers, you can develop healthier coping strategies and avoid unnecessary expenses.

Action Step:

Keep a spending journal for one week. Write down:

- What you purchased.
- Why you made the purchase (e.g., hunger, excitement, stress).
- How you felt afterward (e.g., satisfied, regretful, indifferent).

Look for patterns and adjust your habits accordingly.

The Benefits of Mindful Money Habits

By implementing these small daily practices and tracking your spending without stress, you'll begin to notice significant changes in your financial life:

1. **Increased Awareness:** You'll have a clearer understanding of where your money is going.
2. **Improved Control:** You'll feel empowered to make intentional financial decisions.
3. **Reduced Stress:** Simple, consistent habits eliminate the overwhelm of financial management.
4. **Steady Progress:** Small actions compound over time, leading to meaningful results.

Actionable Steps to Start Today

1. **Adopt One Daily Habit:** Choose one small practice (e.g., daily money check-ins) and commit to it for the next seven days.
2. **Simplify Your Tracking:** Pick a tracking method that feels manageable, and start categorizing your expenses.
3. **Reflect on Emotional Triggers:** Begin identifying the emotions behind your spending and make adjustments.
4. **Automate Savings:** Set up an automatic transfer to your savings account to ensure consistent progress.

Mindful money habits are the cornerstone of financial success. They may seem small and inconsequential at first, but their cumulative effect is profound. With each conscious decision, you move closer to a life of financial freedom and abundance.

Chapter 3: Investing with Intention

Basics of Mindful Investing and Aligning Investments with Personal Values

Investing is one of the most effective ways to grow wealth over time, but it's more than just numbers on a chart or decisions driven by financial gain. Mindful investing involves aligning your investments with your financial goals and personal values, ensuring that every dollar you invest reflects who you are and what you stand for. In this chapter, we'll cover the basics of investing with intention and explore how to align your portfolio with your values, creating a financial future that's both prosperous and meaningful.

The Basics of Mindful Investing

Mindful investing isn't just about picking the "right" stocks or chasing high returns; it's about approaching investments with purpose, clarity, and a long-term perspective. Here's what you need to know to get started:

1. Understand the Purpose of Investing

At its core, investing is about putting your money to work to achieve future goals. Whether it's building an emergency fund, securing retirement, or funding your child's education, your investments should align with your unique aspirations.

Key Questions to Reflect On:

- What are my financial goals, both short-term and long-term?
- How much risk am I comfortable taking to achieve these goals?
- What kind of legacy or impact do I want my investments to leave?

Action Step: Write down your top three financial goals and the timeline for achieving each. These will serve as the foundation for your investment strategy.

2. Know Your Investment Options

Understanding the various types of investments is crucial to making informed decisions. Here's an overview of the most common options:

- **Stocks:** Ownership in a company. High risk but potentially high returns.
- **Bonds:** Loans to companies or governments. Lower risk with steady, predictable returns.
- **Mutual Funds and ETFs:** Collections of stocks or bonds, offering diversification with a single purchase.
- **Real Estate:** Physical property investments, which can provide income and appreciation.
- **Cryptocurrency:** Digital currencies with high volatility and potential rewards.
- **Alternative Investments:** Commodities, hedge funds, or private equity, often requiring specialized knowledge.

Action Step: Research each investment type to understand its risks, benefits, and how it fits into your financial goals.

3. Create a Diversified Portfolio

A diversified portfolio spreads your investments across different asset classes to reduce risk. Mindful investing isn't about putting all your money in one basket but about balancing risk and reward in alignment with your goals.

Basic Principles of Diversification:

- Mix asset classes (e.g., stocks, bonds, real estate).
- Invest across industries (e.g., technology, healthcare, finance).
- Consider geographic diversification (e.g., domestic vs. international investments).

Action Step: Use an online portfolio calculator or consult a financial advisor to create a balanced investment mix.

4. Stay Consistent and Patient

Investing is a long-term game. Markets fluctuate, and short-term volatility can be unnerving, but mindful investors remain calm and focused on their goals.

Action Step:

- Set up automatic contributions to your investment accounts to ensure consistency.
- Avoid impulsive decisions driven by market panic or hype.

Aligning Investments with Personal Values

Mindful investing goes beyond financial returns—it's about ensuring your investments align with your ethical, social, and environmental values. This approach, often called *socially responsible investing (SRI)* or *environmental, social, and governance (ESG)* investing, allows you to grow wealth while making a positive impact.

1. Define Your Core Values

Start by identifying what matters most to you. Consider values like:

- Environmental sustainability
- Social equity
- Corporate ethics
- Community impact

Action Step: Create a list of your top five values and use them as a guide when evaluating investment opportunities.

2. Research ESG and SRI Options

Many funds and companies are specifically designed to align with certain values. ESG metrics evaluate how companies manage environmental, social, and governance issues, while SRI focuses on excluding industries that conflict with ethical principles (e.g., tobacco, fossil fuels, or weapons).

Examples of ESG/SRI Investments:

- **Green Bonds:** Investments in environmentally friendly projects.
- **Sustainable ETFs:** Funds that prioritize companies with strong ESG performance.
- **Impact Investing:** Investments aimed at generating positive social or environmental change alongside financial returns.

Action Step: Use online tools like Morningstar's ESG ratings or platforms like Sustainalytics to evaluate the ethical and environmental impact of potential investments.

3. Avoid Value Misalignment

Investments that contradict your personal values can cause internal conflict and undermine your peace of mind. For example, investing in a company with questionable labor practices might yield returns, but it could weigh on your conscience.

Action Step: Before investing, research the business practices of companies or funds. Look for transparency in their operations and alignment with your values.

4. Balance Values with Financial Goals

While aligning investments with your values is important, it's equally crucial to ensure they align with your financial objectives. Strive for a balance that allows you to grow wealth while staying true to your principles.

Key Considerations:

- Does this investment meet my risk tolerance and return expectations?
- Will it help me achieve my financial goals within the desired timeframe?
- Does it align with my ethical and social values?

The Benefits of Investing with Intention

By combining mindful investing practices with value alignment, you create a strategy that is both financially rewarding and personally fulfilling. Benefits include:

- **Financial Growth:** Long-term wealth accumulation through consistent, informed investment practices.
- **Peace of Mind:** Confidence that your investments reflect your principles.
- **Positive Impact:** Contributing to causes and companies that align with your values.

Actionable Steps to Begin Intentional Investing Today

1. **Clarify Your Goals:** Write down your financial objectives and timeline.
2. **Define Your Values:** Identify the principles that matter most to you.
3. **Research Options:** Explore ESG/SRI funds or companies that align with your values.
4. **Create a Portfolio:** Build a diversified mix of investments tailored to your goals and risk tolerance.
5. **Stay Educated:** Regularly review and adjust your investments to stay aligned with your evolving goals and values.

Investing with intention transforms your financial journey into something much greater than the pursuit of wealth. It becomes a reflection of your beliefs, a vehicle for creating change, and a testament to the power of mindful decision-making.

Chapter 4: The Power of Financial Gratitude

How Gratitude Attracts More Wealth and Builds an Abundance Mindset

Gratitude is often viewed as a feel-good emotion or a polite response to kindness, but when applied to your financial life, it becomes a transformative force. Financial gratitude shifts your focus from scarcity and lack to abundance and opportunity, creating a mental and emotional environment that attracts wealth. In this chapter, we'll explore how gratitude enhances your financial journey and how building an abundance mindset can unlock your potential to create and sustain wealth.

How Gratitude Attracts More Wealth

Gratitude is more than just a fleeting feeling—it's a practice that changes the way you perceive and interact with the world. When you adopt gratitude in your financial life, you tap into its power to reframe challenges, amplify opportunities, and magnetize abundance.

1. Gratitude Reframes Scarcity into Opportunity

It's easy to focus on what you don't have: debts, unmet financial goals, or the pressure of rising expenses. Gratitude flips this script by drawing your attention to what you do have, creating a foundation for growth.

Example:

- Scarcity Mindset: "I don't have enough money to invest."
- Gratitude Mindset: "I'm grateful for the income I have and the small steps I can take to build wealth."

This shift not only reduces stress but also empowers you to find creative solutions.

Action Step:

Each evening, write down three things you're grateful for about your finances, no matter how small they may seem. For example:

- "I'm thankful for my ability to pay my rent this month."
- "I'm grateful for learning new skills that increase my earning potential."
- "I appreciate the unexpected refund I received."

2. Gratitude Strengthens Your Financial Discipline

When you're grateful for your financial resources, you're more likely to use them wisely. Gratitude instills a sense of responsibility and encourages thoughtful spending, saving, and investing.

Action Step:

Before making a purchase, pause to express gratitude for the money you're about to spend. Ask yourself:

- Does this purchase align with my financial goals?
- Am I using my resources in a way that honors the effort I put into earning them?

3. Gratitude Enhances Your Relationships with Money

For many, money can be a source of anxiety or conflict. Gratitude transforms your relationship with money from one of stress to one of appreciation and respect, fostering a sense of peace and confidence.

Action Step:

Create a gratitude mantra related to money, such as:

- "I am grateful for the opportunities money provides."
- "Money flows to me easily and abundantly, and I use it wisely."

Repeat this mantra daily to strengthen your positive association with money.

4. Gratitude Attracts Opportunities

A grateful mindset makes you more attuned to opportunities for growth. When you focus on abundance rather than lack, you're more likely to notice and act on chances to improve your financial situation.

Example:

Someone with a scarcity mindset might dismiss a side hustle as "not worth the effort," while someone with a gratitude mindset sees it as an exciting opportunity to earn and learn.

Action Step:

At the end of each week, reflect on one new financial opportunity that arose and express gratitude for it, whether you acted on it or not.

Building an Abundance Mindset

An abundance mindset goes hand in hand with gratitude. It's the belief that there's enough wealth, success, and opportunity to go around—and that you are fully capable of accessing it. Cultivating this mindset is essential for attracting and sustaining financial prosperity.

1. Recognize Limiting Beliefs About Abundance

The first step in building an abundance mindset is identifying the scarcity-driven beliefs that hold you back, such as:

- "There's never enough money."
- "I'll always struggle financially."
- "If someone else succeeds, there's less for me."

These beliefs create a mental ceiling on your potential, but they can be replaced with empowering alternatives.

Action Step:

Write down one limiting belief about money and reframe it into a statement of abundance. For example:

- Limiting Belief: "I'll never have enough to retire."
- Reframed Belief: "Every step I take brings me closer to a comfortable retirement."

2. Practice Daily Affirmations

Positive affirmations are a powerful tool for rewiring your brain to focus on abundance. By repeating affirmations daily, you train your subconscious mind to believe in your capacity to create and attract wealth.

Examples of Abundance Affirmations:

- "Money flows freely and easily into my life."
- "I am open to receiving unexpected financial blessings."
- "I create value in the world, and I am rewarded abundantly."

Action Step:

Choose one or two affirmations that resonate with you and repeat them each morning and evening.

3. Focus on Giving

An abundance mindset thrives on the principle of giving. When you give—whether it's your time, knowledge, or money—you reinforce the belief that there's more than enough to share.

Action Step:

Set aside a small portion of your income or time for giving. This could be donating to a cause you care about, helping a friend, or mentoring someone.

4. Surround Yourself with Abundance-Minded People

The people you interact with shape your beliefs and attitudes. Surround yourself with individuals who embody abundance, positivity, and financial wisdom.

Action Step:

Join a community or group focused on financial growth, such as personal finance meetups, online forums, or investment clubs. Engage in conversations that inspire and uplift you.

5. Visualize Abundance

Visualization is a powerful way to align your thoughts and actions with an abundance mindset. By vividly imagining your financial goals, you program your brain to seek out opportunities and solutions.

Action Step:

Spend five minutes each day visualizing your financial success. Picture your goals as already achieved:

- See yourself living debt-free.
- Imagine enjoying the freedom to travel or pursue your passions.
- Visualize the positive impact your wealth has on others.

The Benefits of Financial Gratitude and an Abundance Mindset

When gratitude and an abundance mindset become integral to your financial life, you unlock a host of benefits:

1. **Enhanced Resilience:** Challenges feel less overwhelming when you focus on the positive aspects of your financial situation.
2. **Increased Creativity:** A mindset of abundance fosters innovative thinking and problem-solving.
3. **Improved Relationships:** Gratitude and abundance attract supportive, like-minded people into your life.
4. **Sustainable Wealth:** By appreciating and respecting your resources, you build a foundation for long-term prosperity.

Actionable Steps to Harness the Power of Financial Gratitude

1. **Start a Gratitude Journal:** Each day, write down three financial things you're grateful for.
2. **Adopt Abundance Affirmations:** Repeat positive statements about wealth daily.
3. **Reframe Limiting Beliefs:** Replace scarcity-driven thoughts with empowering alternatives.
4. **Visualize Your Goals:** Spend time imagining your financial success as if it's already achieved.
5. **Focus on Giving:** Commit to sharing your resources in ways that align with your values.

Gratitude and abundance are not just attitudes—they are practices that transform your relationship with money. By consistently focusing

on what you have and what's possible, you create an environment where
wealth flows naturally and effortlessly.

Chapter 5: Creating a Wealth Legacy

Planning for Long-Term Financial Stability and Sharing Wealth While Giving Back

Wealth is not just about what you accumulate during your lifetime—it's about the legacy you leave behind. A wealth legacy ensures your financial achievements continue to benefit future generations, your community, and the causes you care about. In this chapter, we will explore how to plan for long-term financial stability and use your resources to make a meaningful impact through sharing and giving back.

Planning for Long-Term Financial Stability

Building a financial legacy begins with creating a robust plan for long-term stability. This involves protecting your assets, ensuring sustainable growth, and preparing for the inevitable transitions of life.

1. Establishing a Clear Vision for Your Legacy

A wealth legacy starts with defining your goals and values. What do you want your financial success to achieve beyond your lifetime? Your vision will guide your decisions and ensure your wealth aligns with your personal principles.

Key Questions to Reflect On:

- How do I want to be remembered financially?
- What values or causes do I want to support with my wealth?
- What resources do I want to leave for my family or community?

Action Step: Write a personal wealth legacy statement outlining your goals, values, and the impact you wish to have.

2. Building an Estate Plan

An estate plan ensures your wealth is distributed according to your wishes. It protects your assets, minimizes taxes, and provides clarity for your loved ones.

Essential Components of an Estate Plan:

- **Will:** A legal document specifying how your assets will be distributed.
- **Trusts:** Tools to manage and protect wealth for specific beneficiaries or causes.
- **Power of Attorney:** Appoints someone to manage your finances if you're unable to do so.
- **Health Care Directive:** Outlines your medical wishes in case of incapacity.

Action Step: Consult an estate planning attorney to draft or update your estate plan. Ensure it reflects your current financial situation and legacy goals.

3. Diversifying Investments for Generational Wealth

Diversification isn't just a strategy for short-term stability; it's a cornerstone of creating generational wealth. By spreading investments across various asset classes, you reduce risk and increase the likelihood of sustainable growth over time.

Examples of Diversified Assets for Legacy Planning:

- Real estate holdings that generate passive income.
- Long-term stock market investments.
- Bonds or fixed-income securities for stability.
- Businesses or entrepreneurial ventures.

Action Step: Review your portfolio with a financial advisor to ensure it's structured for long-term growth and stability.

4. Preparing Future Generations

Wealth preservation depends on equipping your heirs with the knowledge and skills to manage it responsibly.

Ways to Educate the Next Generation:

- Teach financial literacy early, covering topics like budgeting, saving, and investing.
- Share the story of your financial journey, including successes and lessons learned.
- Establish a family mission statement to align everyone with shared values and goals.

Action Step: Schedule regular family meetings to discuss financial topics, goals, and the principles behind your wealth legacy.

Sharing Wealth and Giving Back

While planning for long-term financial stability is essential, creating a wealth legacy also involves using your resources to make a positive impact in the present. Sharing wealth and giving back not only enriches your community but also deepens your sense of purpose and fulfillment.

1. The Philosophy of Giving Back

Giving back is an acknowledgment that wealth is not an isolated achievement but the result of opportunities, support, and contributions from others. It's a way to pay it forward and amplify the impact of your success.

Benefits of Giving Back:

- Strengthens community ties and creates a positive ripple effect.
- Builds a legacy of generosity and compassion.
- Provides personal fulfillment by aligning your financial actions with your values.

2. Strategic Philanthropy

Philanthropy isn't just about writing checks; it's about making intentional, impactful contributions to causes you care about.

Steps to Strategic Giving:

1. **Identify Your Causes:** Focus on issues or organizations that resonate with your values.
2. **Set a Budget:** Allocate a specific percentage of your income or assets for charitable contributions.
3. **Choose the Right Method:** Decide whether to donate directly, establish a foundation, or contribute to donor-advised funds.
4. **Measure Impact:** Track how your contributions are used and the results they achieve.

Action Step: Research charities or nonprofits that align with your values and set up a recurring donation or partnership.

3. Creating Community Impact

Beyond monetary contributions, consider ways to use your time, skills, and network to create a broader impact.

Examples of Non-Monetary Giving:

- Volunteering your expertise to mentor or train others.
- Advocating for policies that support underserved communities.
- Hosting events or workshops to empower others financially.

Action Step: Dedicate one day each month to a community activity, such as volunteering, mentoring, or supporting a local cause.

4. Inspiring Others Through Generosity

One of the most powerful ways to create a wealth legacy is to inspire others to adopt a mindset of generosity. By leading through example, you encourage a culture of giving that extends beyond your immediate contributions.

Ways to Inspire Generosity:

- Share your giving journey publicly to raise awareness for important causes.
- Involve your family and friends in charitable activities.
- Celebrate and amplify the efforts of others who give back.

Action Step: Create a family giving tradition, such as an annual holiday donation drive or volunteering together at a local nonprofit.

The Intersection of Stability and Generosity

A true wealth legacy balances financial stability with generosity. While it's essential to secure your future and provide for your family, sharing your wealth in meaningful ways ensures your success creates a broader, lasting impact.

Benefits of a Balanced Approach:

- Your financial goals are met without sacrificing opportunities to give back.
- You inspire the next generation to value both wealth creation and social responsibility.
- You create a legacy that reflects not just what you achieved, but who you are.

Actionable Steps to Create Your Wealth Legacy

1. **Define Your Legacy Vision:** Write a statement outlining your financial and philanthropic goals.
2. **Create an Estate Plan:** Consult a professional to ensure your assets are protected and distributed according to your wishes.
3. **Diversify Your Portfolio:** Focus on investments that support long-term stability and growth.
4. **Educate Future Generations:** Teach financial literacy and share your wealth journey with your family.
5. **Commit to Giving Back:** Identify causes that resonate with you and set up recurring contributions or volunteer activities.

A wealth legacy is about more than accumulating assets—it's about creating a ripple effect of positivity, stability, and opportunity for those who follow. By planning for long-term financial stability and sharing your wealth generously, you craft a legacy that stands the test of time.

Appendix A: Financial Mindfulness Worksheets and Resources

This appendix serves as a practical guide to help you implement the concepts of financial mindfulness covered in the book. It includes worksheets, templates, and curated resources to support your journey toward building wealth, fostering gratitude, and aligning your finances with your values. Use these tools regularly to stay organized, focused, and intentional about your financial growth.

Worksheet 1: Daily Money Check-In

Purpose: To promote daily mindfulness about your financial situation.

Date: _______________________

1. **Current Account Balance: $_____________**
2. **Recent Transactions (last 3):**
3. **Today's Financial Goal:**
4. **One Thing I'm Grateful for Financially Today:**

Worksheet 2: Financial Gratitude Journal

Purpose: To cultivate gratitude and reframe your relationship with money.

| **Day/Date:** _________________ |

Today's Financial Wins (small or big):

One Positive Action I Took Today for My Finances:

Reflection:

How did practicing gratitude today change my perspective?

Worksheet 3: Monthly Budget Template

Purpose: To align your spending and saving with your financial goals.

Income Sources	Amount
Primary Income	$_________
Side Hustles	$_________
Other Income (e.g., dividends)	$_________
Total Income	$_________

Expense Categories	Budgeted Amount	Actual Amount
Housing (rent/mortgage)	$_________	$_________
Utilities	$_________	$_________
Groceries	$_________	$_________
Transportation	$_________	$_________
Savings/Investments	$_________	$_________
Discretionary Spending	$_________	$_________
Other	$_________	$_________
Total Expenses	$_________	$_________

Reflection Questions:

- Did I stay within my budget this month?
- What categories need adjustment?
- What savings milestones did I achieve?

Worksheet 4: Financial Goals Tracker

Purpose: To monitor your progress toward financial goals.

Goal	Target Amount	Deadline	Current Progress	Steps to Achieve
Emer- gency Fund	$______ __	________	$______ __	________ __________ __________ ________
Pay Off Debt	$______ __	________	$______ __	__________ __________ __________ ________
Save for Vacation	$______ __	________	$______ __	__________ __________ __________ ________
Invest in Retirement	$______ __	________	$______ __	__________ __________ __________ ________

Reflection:

- What milestone am I most proud of this month?
- What challenges did I face, and how can I overcome them moving forward?

Worksheet 5: Values-Based Spending Reflection
Purpose: To align your spending habits with your personal values.

1. **List Your Core Values (e.g., sustainability, family, education):**
2. **Recent Purchases (last 5):**
3. **Reflection Questions:**
    ◦ Do these purchases reflect my values? Why or why not?
    ◦ What changes can I make to ensure my spending aligns with my principles?

Curated Resources for Financial Mindfulness
Books and Literature:

1. *Your Money or Your Life* by Vicki Robin and Joe Dominguez – A guide to transforming your relationship with money.
2. *The Barefoot Investor* by Scott Pape – A practical approach to managing finances with mindfulness and simplicity.
3. *Atomic Habits* by James Clear – While not directly about money, this book helps build lasting habits that can be applied to financial practices.

Online Tools and Apps:

1. **Mint:** For tracking expenses and setting budgets.
2. **YNAB (You Need A Budget):** Helps you allocate every dollar and stay on top of financial goals.
3. **Personal Capital:** Ideal for tracking investments and overall net worth.
4. **GoodBudget:** An app for envelope-based budgeting.

Podcasts:

1. *Afford Anything* with Paula Pant – Focuses on financial independence and intentional spending.
2. *The Minimalists Podcast* – Explores how simplifying life can improve financial health.
3. *Smart Passive Income* with Pat Flynn – Offers advice on generating additional income streams.

Websites:

1. **Investopedia:** Comprehensive resources on investing and personal finance.
2. **NerdWallet:** Comparison tools for credit cards, loans, and financial products.
3. **Mr. Money Mustache:** A blog dedicated to financial independence and frugal living.

Community Groups and Forums:

1. **Reddit's r/PersonalFinance:** A community offering tips and discussions on financial topics.
2. **Bogleheads:** A forum focused on low-cost, long-term investing.
3. **Facebook Groups:** Search for local or online financial literacy and mindfulness groups.

How to Use This Appendix

- Incorporate these worksheets into your daily, weekly, and monthly routines to build mindful financial habits.
- Use the curated resources to deepen your understanding and find tools that resonate with your goals.
- Regularly revisit your goals and reflections to track progress and stay aligned with your financial vision.

By using these resources consistently, you'll develop a strong foundation of financial mindfulness, empowering you to create and sustain wealth with purpose and intention. This appendix is designed to be your practical companion on the journey to financial well-being.

<u>Message from the Author</u>:

I hope you enjoyed this book, I love astrology and knew there was not a book such as this out on the shelf. I love metaphysical items as well. Please check out my other books:

-Life of Government Benefits

-My life of Hell

-My life with Hydrocephalus

-Red Sky

-World Domination:Woman's rule

-World Domination:Woman's Rule 2: The War

-Life and Banishment of Apophis: book 1

-The Kidney Friendly Diet

-The Ultimate Hemp Cookbook

-Creating a Dispensary(legally)

-Cleanliness throughout life: the importance of showering from childhood to adulthood.

-Strong Roots: The Risks of Overcoddling children

-Hemp Horoscopes: Cosmic Insights and Earthly Healing

- Celestial Hemp Navigating the Zodiac: Through the Green Cosmos

-Astrological Hemp: Aligning The Stars with Earth's Ancient Herb

-The Astrological Guide to Hemp: Stars, Signs, and Sacred Leaves

-Green Growth: Innovative Marketing Strategies for your Hemp Products and Dispensary

-Cosmic Cannabis

-Astrological Munchies

-Henry The Hemp

-Zodiacal Roots: The Astrological Soul Of Hemp

- **Green Constellations: Intersection of Hemp and Zodiac**

-Hemp in The Houses: An astrological Adventure Through The Cannabis Galaxy

-Galactic Ganja Guide

Heavenly Hemp
Zodiac Leaves
Doctor Who Astrology
Cannastrology
Stellar Satvias and Cosmic Indicas
<u>Celestial Cannabis: A Zodiac Journey</u>
AstroHerbology: The Sky and The Soil: Volume 1
AstroHerbology:Celestial Cannabis:Volume 2
Cosmic Cannabis Cultivation
The Starry Guide to Herbal Harmony: Volume 1
The Starry Guide to Herbal Harmony: Cannabis Universe: Volume
2

Yugioh Astrology: Astrological Guide to Deck, Duels and more
Nightmare Mansion: Echoes of The Abyss
Nightmare Mansion 2: Legacy of Shadows
Nightmare Mansion 3: Shadows of the Forgotten
Nightmare Mansion 4: Echoes of the Damned
The Life and Banishment of Apophis: Book 2
Nightmare Mansion: Halls of Despair
<u>Healing with Herb: Cannabis and Hydrocephalus</u>
<u>Planetary Pot: Aligning with Astrological Herbs: Volume 1</u>
Fast Track to Freedom: 30 Days to Financial Independence Using AI, Assets, and Agile Hustles
<u>Cosmic Hemp Pathways</u>
How to Become Financially Free in 30 Days: 10,000 Paths to Prosperity
Zodiacal Herbage: Astrological Insights: Volume 1
Nightmare Mansion: Whispers in the Walls
The Daleks Invade Atlantis
Henry the hemp and Hydrocephalus

10X The Kidney Friendly Diet
Cannabis Universe: Adult coloring book

Hemp Astrology: The Healing Power of the Stars

Zodiacal Herbage: Astrological Insights: Cannabis Universe: Volume 2

<u>Planetary Pot: Aligning with Astrological Herbs: Cannabis Universes: Volume 2</u>

Doctor Who Meets the Replicators and SG-1: The Ultimate Battle for Survival

Nightmare Mansion: Curse of the Blood Moon

<u>The Celestial Stoner: A Guide to the Zodiac</u>

Cosmic Pleasures: Sex Toy Astrology for Every Sign

Hydrocephalus Astrology: Navigating the Stars and Healing Waters

Lapis and the Mischievous Chocolate Bar

Celestial Positions: Sexual Astrology for Every Sign

Apophis's Shadow Work Journal: : A Journey of Self-Discovery and Healing

Kinky Cosmos: Sexual Kink Astrology for Every Sign

Digital Cosmos: The Astrological Digimon Compendium

Stellar Seeds: The Cosmic Guide to Growing with Astrology

Apophis's Daily Gratitude Journal

Cat Astrology: Feline Mysteries of the Cosmos

The Cosmic Kama Sutra: An Astrological Guide to Sexual Positions

Unleash Your Potential: A Guided Journal Powered by AI Insights

Whispers of the Enchanted Grove

Cosmic Pleasures: An Astrological Guide to Sexual Kinks

369, 12 Manifestation Journal

Whisper of the nocturne journal(blank journal for writing or drawing)

The Boogey Book

Locked In Reflection: A Chastity Journey Through Locktober

Generating Wealth Quickly:

How to Generate $100,000 in 24 Hours

Star Magic: Harness the Power of the Universe

The Flatulence Chronicles: A Fart Journal for Self-Discovery

The Doctor and The Death Moth

Seize the Day: A Personal Seizure Tracking Journal

The Ultimate Boogeyman Safari: A Journey into the Boogie World and Beyond

Whispers of Samhain: 1,000 Spells of Love, Luck, and Lunar Magic: Samhain Spell Book

Apophis's guides:

Witch's Spellbook Crafting Guide for Halloween

<u>**Frost & Flame: The Enchanted Yule Grimoire of 1000 Winter Spells**</u>

<u>**The Ultimate Boogey Goo Guide & Spooky Activities for Halloween Fun**</u>

Harmony of the Scales: A Libra's Spellcraft for Balance and Beauty

The Enchanted Advent: 36 Days of Christmas Wonders

Nightmare Mansion: The Labyrinth of Screams

Harvest of Enchantment: 1,000 Spells of Gratitude, Love, and Fortune for Thanksgiving

The Boogey Chronicles: A Journal of Nightly Encounters and Shadowy Secrets

The 12 Days of Financial Freedom: A Step-by-Step Christmas Countdown to Transform Your Finances

Sigil of the Eternal Spiral Blank Journal

A Christmas Feast: Timeless Recipes for Every Meal

Holiday Stress-Free Solutions: A Survival Guide to Thriving During the Festive Season

Yu-Gi-Oh! Holiday Gifting Mastery: The Ultimate Guide for Fans and Newcomers Alike

Holiday Harmony: A Hydrocephalus Survival Guide for the Festive Season

Celestial Craft: The Witch's Almanac for 2025 – A Cosmic Guide to Manifestations, Moons, and Mystical Events

Doctor Who: The Toymaker's Winter Wonderland

Tulsa King Unveiled: A Thrilling Guide to Stallone's Mafia Masterpiece

Pendulum Craft: A Complete Guide to Crafting and Using Personalized Divination Tools

Nightmare Mansion: Santa's Eternal Eve

Starlight Noel: A Cosmic Journey through Christmas Mysteries

The Dark Architect: Unlocking the Blueprint of Existence

Surviving the Embrace: The Ultimate Guide to Encounters with The Hugging Molly

The Enchanted Codex: Secrets of the Craft for Witches, Wiccans, and Pagans

Harvest of Gratitude: A Complete Thanksgiving Guide

Yuletide Essentials: A Complete Guide to an Authentic and Magical Christmas

Celestial Smokes: A Cosmic Guide to Cigars and Astrology

Living in Balance: A Comprehensive Survival Guide to Thriving with Diabetes Insipidus

Cosmic Symbiosis: The Venom Zodiac Chronicles

The Cursed Paw of Ambition

Cosmic Symbiosis: The Astrological Venom Journal

Celestial Wonders Unfold: A Stargazer's Guide to the Cosmos (2024-2029)

The Ultimate Black Friday Prepper's Guide: Mastering Shopping Strategies and Savings

Cosmic Sales: The Astrological Guide to Black Friday Shopping

Legends of the Corn Mother and Other Harvest Myths

Whispers of the Harvest: The Corn Mother's Journal

The Evergreen Spellbook

The Doctor Meets the Boogeyman

The White Witch of Rose Hall's SpellBook

The Gingerbread Golem's Shadow: A Study in Sweet Darkness

The Gingerbread Golem Codex: An Academic Exploration of Sweet Myths

The Gingerbread Golem Grimoire: Sweet Magicks and Spells for the Festive Witch

The Curse of the Gingerbread Golem

10-minute Christmas Crafts for kids

<u>Christmas Crisis Solutions: The Ultimate Last-Minute Survival Guide</u>

Gingerbread Golem Recipes: Holiday Treats with a Magical Twist

The Infinite Key: Unlocking Mystical Secrets of the Ages

Enchanted Yule: A Wiccan and Pagan Guide to a Magical and Memorable Season

Dinosaurs of Power: Unlocking Ancient Magick

Astro-Dinos: The Cosmic Guide to Prehistoric Wisdom

Gallifrey's Yule Logs: A Festive Doctor Who Cookbook

The Dino Grimoire: Secrets of Prehistoric Magick

The Gift They Never Knew They Needed

The Gingerbread Golem's Culinary Alchemy: Enchanting Recipes for a Sweetly Dark Feast

A Time Lord Christmas: Holiday Adventures with the Doctor

Krampusproofing Your Home: Defensive Strategies for Yule

Silent Frights: A Collection of Christmas Creepypastas to Chill Your Bones

Santa Raptor's Jolly Carnage: A Dino-Claus Christmas Tale

Prehistoric Palettes: A Dino Wicca Coloring Journey

The Christmas Wishkeeper Chronicles

The Starlight Sleigh: A Holiday Journey

Elf Secrets: The True Magic of the North Pole

Candy Cane Conjurations
Cooking with Kids: Recipes Under 20 Minutes
Doctor Who: The TARDIS Confiscation
The Anxiety First Aid Kit: Quick Tools to Calm Your Mind
Frosty Whispers: A Winter's Tale
The Infinite Key: Unlocking the Secrets to Prosperity, Resilience, and Purpose
The Grasping Void: Why You'll Regret This Purchase
Astrology for Busy Bees: Star Signs Simplified
The Instant Focus Formula: Cut Through the Noise
The Secret Language of Colors: Unlocking the Emotional Codes
Sacred Fossil Chronicles: Blank Journal
The Christmas Cottage Miracle
Feeding Frenzy: Graboid-Inspired Recipes
Manifest in Minutes: The Quick Law of Attraction Guide
The Symbiote Chronicles: Doctor Who's Venomous Journey
Think Tiny, Grow Big: The Minimalist Mindset
The Energy Key: Unlocking Limitless Motivation
New Year, New Magic: Manifesting Your Best Year Yet
Unstoppable You: Mastering Confidence in Minutes
Infinite Energy: The Secret to Never Feeling Drained
Lightning Focus: Mastering the Art of Productivity in a Distracted World
Saturnalia Manifestation Magick: A Guide to Unlocking Abundance During the Solstice
Graboids and Garland: The Ultimate Tremors-Themed Christmas Guide
12 Nights of Holiday Magic
The Power of Pause: 60-Second Mindfulness Practices
The Quick Reset: How to Reclaim Your Life After Burnout
The Shadow Eater: A Tale of Despair and Survival
The Micro-Mastery Method: Transform Your Skills in Just Minutes a Day

If you want solar for your home go here: https://www.harborso-lar.live/apophisenterprises/

Get Some Tarot cards: https://www.makeplayingcards.com/sell/apophis-occult-shop

<u>**Get some shirts: https://www.bonfire.com/store/apophis-shirt-emporium/**</u>

<u>Instagrams:</u>
@apophis_enterprises,
@apophisbookemporium,
@apophisscardshop
Twitter: @apophisenterpr1 Tiktok:@apophisenterprise
Youtube: @sg1fan23477, @FiresideRetreatKingdomTop of
Form
Hive: @sg1fan23477
CheeLee: @SG1fan23477

Podcast: Apophis Chat Zone: https://open.spotify.com/show/5zXbrCLEV2xzCp8ybrfHsk?si=fb4d4fdbdce44dec

Newsletter: https://apophiss-newsletter-27c897.beehiiv.com/

If you want to support me or see posts of other projects that I have come over to: **buymeacoffee.com/mpetchinskg**
I post there daily several times a day

Get your Dinowicca or Christmas themed digital products, especially Santa Raptor songs and other musics. Here: **https://sg1fan23477.gumroad.com**

Apophis Yuletide Digital has not only digital Christmas items, but it will have all things with Dinowicca as well as other Digital products.